ONE-LEGGED POETRY

ONE-LEGGED POETRY

TRAGEDY, POLITICS & A SEA MONSTER

JACKO MONAHAN

Published by BLAST PRESS
324B Matawan Avenue
Cliffwood, NJ 07721
(732) 970-8409
gregglory.com

Library of Congress Control Number: 2017959674

ISBN-13: 978-0998482910
ISBN-10: 0998482919

Author photo by Jared Weeks
Cover drawing by Peter Weller
Cover design by Gregg G. Brown

CONTENTS

ONE-LEGGED POETRY

INTRODUCTION

I'm living on borrowed time. Things happen and time runs faster than us. In 2014, my old tar burns from 1974 became infected cuts that had to be operated on.

While recovering in the next 6 to 8 weeks, I wrote this book based on a sense of urgency. I write mostly free form, and I tried to slow down a little bit and be more comprehensive to the public at large.

At the end of my recovery, I caught a nasty infection behind my knee. A day later, I was put in a medically induced coma and lost my leg.

Only 30% of necrotizing fasciitis victims survive . . . tick tock tick tock.

A year later, while surviving one-leggedness, I went blind . . . tick tock tick tock.

I called Dan Weeks & Gregg G. Brown, my fellow poets and infamous partners in the Brighton Bar/CoJack poetry readings, and I told them I was getting desperate to get published.

After 30 or 40 years putting on and playing approximately 10,000 live original shows w/ bands and poets, I had never slowed down enough to publish my own poems. Thirteen vinyl records, and history was forgetting me!

I decided, even though I was already one-legged, I was in a state of war and survival when this material was written. I considered it to be a complete work while I was writing it. Life is about breaking it down—get to work, get it done.

Bon Appetit

. . . tick tock

tick tock

Jacko Monahan

Palisades Park, N.J.

June 8, 2017

THE POEMS

THE COMMAND OF PAINT

the command of paint
    on plastic shoulders
    an army of prayers
some beautiful standards
    a public inconvenience
screening w/ intensities
    the long suffering incarbonate
1500 mi to the north
    up to our necks in civilization
up in smoke, shrinking dust, feel of,
will you forget me . . . tomorrow
the drugs come off
    we're like the planet's tool
    planted feet, feeling prey
scrolling mantlepiece of shrunken heads
gotta fit someplace
    in the intel-ference
    intolerance, subjugation
weird ghost walks
    swollen parapets

sweet orchestrations
    bell notes, drumbeats
diabetic pinch pts., . . . penis included
    needlework on the wall

NOT, AS IF

crackling hashtags, google up . . . or
    as if socialized media would provide, said, as such
    for all humanity, in more than name only
I wrote a letter, rode horses w/ my daughter
sent her off to the highlands
    I see-saw the sweltering
accidental responsibility
    this continuity @ home in the henhouse
mother's day,
    kick-off returns contribute
college is higher education & more than tuition
crisis sobriety,
    repatriate, if abducted
    freedom, if enslaved
    empower, if incorporated
monkey bar, swing set, billy goat's gruff
    drowned in a superstorm
fracked by filiality, socialized insurances
    this care is on the southside
    this tweeting is f/ the birds, nomenclature idiomized

I've got ice on burns
    bandaged wounds of time
honeysuckle rose, sweetie, pumpkin pie, the swimmer swims
gestated in the zeitgeist, who wrote this what, when, where
transcend the enormous
    the eternity of parenting
but energy can neither be created nor destroyed, maybe
reincarnated, reborn
or pointlessly computerized in the thermo-nucleic armageddons

OUR QUEST

I miss... dancing jigs
I miss... shoveling snow
I miss... praising the lord
begging forgiveness
    for unforgivable sins
carrying on endlessly
    about things I forgot to do

I miss... booking bands
I miss... bouncing balls
I miss... chopping wood
I miss... talking about politics
comic-con, come easy
walking amongst all my old stuff
disorganized chaos
    as if I could inherit the wind

I miss... traveling light
I miss... going where I shouldn't
I miss... being free to sky the limit

overgrown w/ what's due...
a remunerated glory sown
that last diamond
across an ocean
one world @ a time
what must be done
before we die

AS IF I COULD SAVE THE WORLD

40 yrs of tar burns,
    fish scales & ruffled feathers
21, baccarat, 007
    my mission is to accomplish
what others fail . . . to care less about
whispering about pop culture
    the minions of ex-communication
a microbrew in the making
a van gogh on the banks of a never-never land
1st and goal in the 4th 1/4 inside the 10
    the #'s don't lie, even if . . .
you're @ a loss forwards
you got in for free anyway
    loaded for bear, endangered species
the whales are watching
even if god seems blind to the continued injustices

RESERVE AND CONTEMPLATE

never on a limb???
    how'd you get to be a bird???
all that free wheeling
    time on a bench, back to the wall
the river rushing by while
    mushrooms are grown in the dark
the static nature of contemporary politics
the tried and true juxtapositionary
the hardwood of rare breed
    antibiotics, murals, eternities
everything in its place . . . behave yourself
    3-D chess . . . @ its best
even my very own mollyhood
    may the roads rise to meet her
sometimes I think I'm in excelsior
    as the standards move up on the hill
steak on a plate . . . .
    you bet I overheard that!
pain in the ass,
    like opinions, everybody's got one

playing ball in high cotton
    supersonics, jubilee, hail marys
like caesar, copernicus, galileo
      you might as well throw it out there
      you've got nothing better to do
than contemplate the universe
      and, on a higher note . . . be @ 1 w/ it

WHAT'S BLINKING

happy TV
    death to the masses
w/ or w/o training wheels
    lockjaw, traffic jams, curses, curses, curses
bad actors
    who don't even bother with their lines
know how to drop an expletive
your rap's not tight
      your pants don't fit,
who knew?
    —the stupidest lines
would be repeated ad infinitum
    collusion, extortion, uxorial
this bomb of a weather report
the last message
    before the disappearances
calling all cars
    bring me some clothes
your reputation proceeds you now
    billings, fresh produce, rapture

you better watch your p's and q's
    god is even in your underwear
yes, you got jokes,
    but nobody's laughing @ deviltry
spit shine, drill revue, quarter bounce
barracks full of rough and ready shock troopers
    don't change the channel
it's showtime!!!

TO THE SOUND
OF A CRESCENDO
OF CRASHING CYMBALS

I'm the type
    that's gotta be doing
    2 things @ once
    just to keep myself occupied
like suffering succotash
    and whistling dixie
like rubbing alcohol & metaformin
    working on my dietary proclivity
    and quoting ex-presidents @ ease
just ask anyone
    who ever talked to me
    on the phone, or in person
    if I ever go off topic
not a stargazer but a universal man
who's watching the store?

and where you been all my life?
credit to go, on a mission to mars
    on the same boat w/ my sainted mother
not exactly kosher
    & on line to be a revolutionary
horseback, computerized, alienation
        adopted to prevention tactics
the hack and harry of it all
the alfred e newman bridge to nowhere
a youth foundation of american individualism
a bearded gangsta in a gang of one
    like I was the only contestant
in the cosmic, ever-lovin', whole shebang of a gong show

COSTUME DRAMA
ON PARADE

markets dropping
    pull up your pants
take that ring out of your nose
    overweight puppets sing
all you transgender musketeers
    rubbernecking on out
a delivery uptown by taxi ranking
a credit checking administrator
    missing intelligence dispatches
    eating chicken vindaloo & crackers
parachuting by proxy
    incur the occurrence
    according to the rules
whales, platypus, rhinoceros
under docks, beneath wheels, doctrines shift
fevers to botulism
    occasions of sin

the weight on the calves
    different plights
the socialist's controversies
the negativity conscripts
    but, bet w/ humanity
    not against it
that's the kind of animal you are
    not a robot, an angel
    or the devil in disguise
in a parade that never ends

DANCING ABOUT
THE BEEHIVE

it's a world of opera
    get ready to die
peacefully in the meadow
    too complicated to explain
7 sinners, 6 tool & die men
    4 aces & 5 cuckoos all in a row
abillifying the murderers in the room
I'm all out of time . . . @ twilight
I hear boots & nazi anthems a-coming
    this testament assemblage
it's unpredictable
    what inspires memory on the dime
I'll never remember
    your license-plate #
    my peevish sense of pain
why the light in my eyes
    shines against me, Ø for me

the great minds of the deluge
the colors of prison
    it's one big cartoon, do the math
writing in the dark
    in a demilitarized zone
the sewerage of forensics
the ticker-tape
    parade & swagger
deep falsetto, heard . . .
    when seen . . . believe
and Ø get stung while . . .
dancing about the beehive

A HOSPITAL BED
IN PURGATORY

3 wks. of skepticism...now
    old rock is easy listening
    I'm still my own worst enemy
tar burns of the past
      still debreeding
dormant hopes withheld
    of the non-aggressive prosthetics
once on the cross
    always on the cross
horse and piggyback
boneyard for the good thief
    scarlet detachment
    snoopy in my lap . . . sniveling
teach the priests spanish
teach the preacher gospel
    word will get to one of them
    soccer, sooner, or later

gasping for double entendre
    ventilator, defibrillated
grasp on a boondock
    waterfront, ghetto, cloudy
happy/sad diametrics
    the radial sundial
    the circumference of stay
the zip is coming to get me now
    which came 1st
the chicken or the egg

WHAT'S HOT AND WHAT'S NOT, TODAY —7/24/2014

79° in the shade
   low lying clouds over NYC
   clearing out to the east
I'm betrayed by nurses
   so what, on the caring index
I'm still in love with being alive
I'm sure that's good news . . .
     to the poor & homeless
     to the mets for their away games
lady liberty, the flowers & weeds,
     on the hi-line sanctuary
     on a trade acquisition for
. . . the rangers, the knicks, the giants,
an extreme amount of the ku-klux-klan
     in south, south jersey

in west, west texas
pipeline & oil spill, mafia garbage dumping
over-irradiated plots of land . . .
all over the US of A
off the coast of Japan
in Dubai's stock exchange
for the next governor of NJ
whose got to be a democrat, out of Newark
who won't be part of these chummy
lawyer deals, or part of brittany spears' lingerie line
network, jizzwads, hot topics, sepsis
or other orchestrated bacterial spread
—let me drive you home in the even-ing

SWIFTER THAN A REGRET

don't date the wounded, visions,
don't carry on in public
don't spread the rumors,
    blasting caps to venus . . . veins & viruses
she's got a lean, mean
    karate class, alter-ego, island past
the tribal look
the mountain rangeable
the beautiful waterfall
    shaped eyebrows
    compact demeanor of
heart like a mirror
    culture of stories
higher in the clouds of chaos than . . .
    milked goats, chicken guts
the terms of piracy
the stance of an idle goddess
    slaves of the time & terms
the farming father's
    future in the hills

famous, or famous is as does
the natural ingredients,
ghosts out of pocket expense
mad imagination
it was a dream *ire* regret
what space avails as a ras dub
war of blessings
the flight of future

CONSTIPATED THINKING

shave your beard
    cut off your limbs
get hip-hop abs, itemizable
    customized poverty
the sharks are circling
they are attempting to eat, chum . . .
the remaining krill
    forbidden planet
drug tunnels of immigration
I would probably stop writing
    if I didn't have something
    compelling to say
unforgiving world
    of out of work congresses
    of bring it on coitus
our most amazing offer ever
    purgative cleansers, or not
men with guns
    imbeciles of revenge
who forget how to be aware

retrofitting the asbestos, aluminum, ether
a task reward,
    not a quantitative or quality issue
    to lie in wait and stab the king
bottom feeders; quacks, quirks, quills
    morons on both sides of the fence
shit or get off the pot

MOVING PARTS

I am not of this earth
    the world belongs to everyone else
what I own
    is boxed up & ready to go
incinerator, crematorial, wildfire
    walk-a-mile, trip on over . . . step
take a red-eye, secretarial, nom de guerre
    pin back your ears fromme
if the fish own the ocean???
    why are they beaching themselves?
eyes abroad with detached retinas... seen
ebola in west africa,
    the economics of the ukraine
    the religious exascervations of the gaza strip
zebras won't change stripes
    I still see the other side of people in movies
but subjectivity
    depends on the director, cinematographer, auteur theory
it's not all X's & O's, cooing swans & garter belts
    the meek will inherit the earth

    the aliens, the GMO science, A-bombs & such
it's a dirty job
    but somebody's got to do it
blasting off,
    infinity and beyond . . .
in the flesh; & how about, etc. . . . . pins all
the extras with a donkey's tail!
. . . pin it on

TAUGHT MILK

I'd like to teach the world
   to fish or cut bait
   to barbwire the cattle empire
I sent for you, thought you
   might like to be the next energy tsar
kaopectate, milk of magnesia, ammonium nitrate
callow suspicions,
   take your medicine, jurisprudence of
   the naked and the dead
as you come in the room
   crosstown traffic & monster magnets
the simple plans
   of compass pts. & racial innuendo
time in the hoosegow, big house, uptown
these 4 walls of heavy metals & dioxins
thanks for the ticky-tacky memories of habit
times of weed & Ø money,
   better than of $ & Ø weed
I've got hospitalization
   a barrel full of monkeys

this crazy zoo I call a brainstorm
  bicameral legislation w/ clean bandages
nuts & butter, bitter nuances
nails & screws, bolt action
next available idiot
  of disparate dysfunctionalism
who owns the village & global gluttony of spilt milk

TOO MANY TO CROSS

one stop shopping
   in the drawer & under the table
feathers and flight
   single cell organisms
   survival of the economists & picklers
opposable thumbs bringing home bacon
   thrall, kanaka, neophytes, jurists
how you got to join the club
   citizenship, custodian, turk & cossack
all the marvelous participants
annihilation tactics
   of formal political allies switching
watching the rivers turn red
   biblical torrential gravities en general
the seriousness of things said, wild & vivid
the written on the wind
   all things big & small, even the pee-wee
shelf-life, biodegradable, misfits and mighty
some moves
   you've never seen before

the invisible, pheromones, hob-knobbery
the blind leading painted indians
    you know buoyancy & ballast
a little less blood . . . everyday jesuses
    home improvements y'all, I tell ya
I gotta piss on the yellow side
    and I bled @ the office, while
blending into waves & currents.

AN INDUSTRIALIZED HUMANITY OF ONE

the back, the shoulder, the neck, the rock
the ankles, . . . gin rummy, madre de dios
    a slow ride across the pampas
nevermore . . .
    that chippy raven, horseback, whale rider
all the women, say,
    Ø rubbernecking, nailbiters, flibber-flabbery
scientists prefer
    a constitutional moment
    a headlong diversion
diamonds & pearls, individualism
    the princess & the pea
    the aging prostate, superbetatized
a comfortable solution
    to the daily urge & peck, the I ♥
    to how I remember my mama
a preparation of plausible deniability

read newspapers, cradled responsibility
the afternoons come like rain
the baby ratifies a suitable situation
    . . . direct contact, f/ a grandpappy
stand up & count coup
    warriors of youthful ambition
I hope her armor of love blows away enemies
    & is strong enough to withstand
. . . the heat blast & the elements

ON THE SUNNYSIDE, ACROSS THE OCEAN, BEYOND THE SEEN

no further dalliances are acceptable
    scarface, bucktooth, handsome is, . . . stains
put your pants
    on one leg @ at time, like everyone
eyepatch, crutches, pistols @ dawn
    she's left the nunnery alone in ×
commuters of subway & pathtrain platforms
    strapholders in the realm of the coin
subsidies, bankdraft, parental interference
    a pain of immutable sacrifice
    a dawn of patriotic taxation ticks
scarecrow, carpetbagger, flame retardant
      the general's epaulets
word is bond, right on, right on, brothers & sisters
    my only child is by blood wise spun

a cripple across the seas, becoming
    waterproof, primed, illustrious
a way out of darkness, life's stupidity
    devil killer, vampire hunter, buffer zone
you gotta do. . . .
    whatever you gotta do . . . also,
beekeeper, butterfly, farmhand,
      croppie in the blood
beautiful smile, I remember so well
    how we gonna do this together
tell your mama, it's too true
    the otherside becomes one
when we have faith in dreams, love & each other,
                  as well as family

THOSE WHO WERE
& THOSE WHO CAME

conestoga, wagonwheel,
    across mountain, desert, plain & treeline
we floated up at dawn
    pioneers, frontiersmen, cavalry
we came together,
    but had separate destinies
commanchero, mescalero, breeds
    tribes and nations, sovereignties
@ 1st, we knew
    the ironhorse was coming
but what it brought, we couldn't guess
    . . . as part & parcel of civilized world
race, genocides, all plain & simple
the white eyes, fork-ed tongue,
    . . . never to keep a single treaty, as sacrosanct
a trail of the dead
a trail of tears

w/o a future by any other name
ghost dancer, sun catcher, walkabout
    the outlawed rituals of language & culture
a way of life succumbed to lack of reason
    the last of buffalo, who roamed
provided sustenances
    in the crossfire of heritages
remember those who lived before us
    & from whence they came,
as the class of most of us, in case, we weren't

PHOTOSHOPPING
THE HAPHAZARDOUS IDEA

a desktop,
  full of ticket stubs
a photographic memory
  passports, licenses, airline transfers
no sure way out
  w/o a broken memory, or heart
this came from that or
  because of whom . . . etc.
how we got to missing links, the museum
  of confused information
why a loudspeaker's got answers
  reverberation, echoes
the downtime on the carousel
the wring and ratchet up
the spindle of conglomerate
the great big council, about which
  nobody bothered to re-iterate 2×s

fair warning, full tilt axis, ya dink,
    even evil as a 2nd nature
a delivery of contrivances
what we cobble together as true
bet to a balanced budget
a #ed depth of content
    and all the out of control context
now, put that in your computerized world
    and smoke it,
because the roof is already
on fire and falling in dinky dau . . . sproing!

BOXERS & DRAWERS

dribble & drool
    everybody's talking . . . at me???
about a new way of walking???
makes you want to lose your mind?
obamacare,
    and over, under, sideways down?
legalize the hemp!!!
    most people self-medicate
their way through life anyway already
    druthers and avast ye swabs
hand me a dish towel, swirlies
    pope on a rope, mobilized
    cash door prizes, tips & tabs
the × it took to get uptown . . . xt
the broadway and main st., walls cave in
    principles ad infinitum
tiddly wink, johnny on a pony
    kick the can, shvakes
a last living relative in lithuania
    thanks dracula, ok fido

printed news, booked gig, italics
    soup cans, art craze, mass media
the catch and overflow in a catacomb
    ebola, chikunganya, pimps
an STD to remember me by
and in this corner,
    the will to continue to forget
filthy fowls, dirty birds & milky chicken spit

IN SATAN'S PLACE

there's very little leftover
    once you get to kicking out the jams
motherfuckers, fellow citizens, little sisters
    the good, the bad & the ugly
    the fox in the henhouse
the disorders of a combative nature, the stupids
contraries in dystopia
why you studied french in the 1st place
ennui, existentialism, John Paul Melville
    a whale of a different color
shutters on the beachhouse windows
splinters on the bench & horror show
    an arab in jerusalem, everywhere
once were conquerors
    all were imperialistic capitalist pigs
tie a dog up
    to a stake in the backyard
come out the backdoor
    and kick him on your way home
if you don't make any money that night

displacement of disillusionment
dopey dildo tactics dumbo
cruelty to dumb animals, you know
the sum of all fears, et al.
thus you know what I'm talking abt.
right, Henry the VIII, king vicious
little hilters, old maos, dead stalins
venomous behaviors of gone, and left behind for good, or
better than being in satan's place

THROUGHOUT THE NIGHT

pejorative,
    exploratory surgery
pervasive throughout
    the word, district, politburo
busts and statuesque likenesses
    possible explanations
    for heretical behavioralisms
throughout the lake district
    there might be swamp creatures
bubbly muds
    of little tiny bits and pieces
put a yarn on it
    francs, yen, deutschmarks
bring in the army
control, standards & practices
chevrons & lightbulbs
the prescience of idealism
    I'll still be a warrior of distinction
the bother of survival
    fussy and necessary

and if we ran out of—gas & tools
downright citizenship,
    it might help, our understanding of it all
it might bring some sense & peace
to waking up in the middle of the night
    & signing the message board

HOW TO EXTRAPOLATE

paper dolls
    can't smoke cigars
rich people
    don't pay taxes
a clock on the wall
    strikes the same time
    twice a day
swollen brains & puffed up muscles
so wide awake
    we take gambles
    we rent rooms
and carry on
    like there's no tomorrow
boy, are my arms tired
box cars & snakes eyes
    plans of mice & men
the big scheme of things
the purpose of it all
    slavery is still an issue
cotton picking, industrial workers union

pick-pockets & carpetbaggers
    reconstruction, facsimiles of
ways & means
    the presidential howdy doody
only one way out of here
    in the up & down of it all
it's just cut & paste & paint by #s
    & spin the bottle

LET'S MAKE SOME CALLS

this teflon stick
thought process
the way I write,
    gotta come to something
gotta pay dividends
gotta collect interests
shoulda, woulda, coulda
you was my brudda
you shoulda looked out for me
now what am I???? chopped liver
a 2× loser, w/ a 1 way ticket to . . .
palookaville, smalltime, visionary tactics
    a magic lantern picture show
clairvoyance and purple sound
    a fuzzy, hairy creature tone
one of the great & unwashed many
one of the million stories
    in the naked city
    in the bamboo jungle
an erased blackboard

    of rock around the clock
and hey you, on the floor
let's rock some more
in a town w/o pity
    on a xylophone of wrench
use your imagination
    & let's do a benefit
kiss me maybe, we'll be able
to save everybody's soul . . . together

(PARAPHRASING THE) FINAL CURTAIN CALL

everybody's got to sometime
and you're nobody till somebody loves you
   so what am I . . . chopped liver, pasty guts
   daddy mayhem, the hairy eyeball
a politician w/o a constituency
a veto w/o a bill to pass, gas & oil to go . . .
filibuster, napoleonic, papal bull
another long russian winter
a survivalist, island stowaway
kabuki mask, easter egg, Xmas past
in the river of time,
   I line walls w/ paperworks
   it hides a lot of sins, sticks to shoes
just gru, filly gumbo, duppiedom
just a walking, talking zombie bat
   the 8's on the dime 2 @ a ×
I ain't lyin'. . . lion of judea, rastaman

presta john w/ the arc of the covenant
straight outta compton, mexican jail, tunnel of drugs
    w/ CIA money & an FBI profile
fatal rage motherfucker
    . . . we know you, you'll be back
and I'll bring some blister on it,
on the dark side of the moon, far to the left
    me & Larry almost blew up Pink Floyd & saw Jeff Beck
    on a handtruck—took too many quaaludes
and I'll take 2 dinosaur eggs over easy fried just right, Ø too greasy
so if you ain't got 'em, go out & get 'em
'cause I ain't going till you come back with 'em

DAYBREAKERS

what's with,
    the unbridled optimism of youth
    the justice for all, created equalities
    the blood sugar diabetes f/ breakfast
boot drag in the clamp down, cave drawn
    jail guitar doors, full of colored & poor
the over the border, counterintuitive, parking job
the walls are sticky,
    w/ blood & guts & chemical warfare
the just before you got there, meetings
w/o being told, it was all going on
you ever been on the wrong side of the land laws
    the door slam, or under the glass ceiling bubble wrap
out of gas, dying in a hot sun
    dry spell, camouflage, uniformed army
    drafted, 1st round pick, universal donor
organ transplant, mr. friendly, don't mind if I do
w/o the henpeck & divorcals, all hunchbacked
    a baby boom, baby daddy, tight squeeze
mortgages & interests

hospital bills & insurance
    coverage & such
the beatles had a lot of hits
    Ø all of which they wrote, vampirism
vested interest, darlings of the media control
    an American w/o talent, voice, or
                even a dance to do
skippity-do-da-day y'all
    sometimes, that's just the way it goes

YOU'RE NEVER COMPLETELY
OUT OF THE WOODS

quo vadis,
    whither goes the stranger
the fish are jumping, weepy
    I'm feeling froggy
queasy, maladroit, distanced
    like a druid in the forest
I'm waiting for the sun to come up
    penny dreadful, dime novel
    2 bits & a quarterback,
nickelodeon, dollarstore indian
    stuck needle in a haystack,
      the stars aligned, belly of the beast
      the rituals of becoming
spy vs. spy
    & the songs that rise above
common circumstances
    on the way to a vendetta

vengeance is mine said the lord
    sticky wicket, crumpets, tea & biscuits
crackers in bed
    sex w/ the nearest, closest, available idiot
gladiator combat
    the incidents of cause & effect
we stood in circles . . . and observed
we experience it all 1st hand
    head over heels, the song & dance
the lost art of perspective
in a changing world

BLAME IT ON THE DRUGS

running on mindlessness
    crippled to a hobbling
gasket, geysers,
    shock proof arraignments
a $150 million army
    ebola in a hospital room
a presidential wireless
a shophouse solipsism
    the hairpin turns
 once were respectable
    going down doing the right thing
fracking for opportunities
    not so proud now banky
I misplaced the prerogative
    they made me a criminal
navigator paperboy, a blonde
    follow the money . . . dear sirs,
rappers in love,
    net worth in an elevator,
make nice, you're on TV

tell lies in the schoolyard
     walk up, cold water flat, teahouse
give yourself up to the authorities
gov't, the movement, a painter's song
I'm praying to god
     forgive me in my foxhole
sometimes you just don't know what to say
so blame it on the drugs

UP TO THE LIMITLESS SKY

it could take a bullet
    to convince me . . . cumulus nimbus
a surgical knife,
    blood on blood, et al., etc.
a concerted effort
all in black & white,
    good vs. evil, such as,
and don't hit me,
    w/ that ugly stick
I'm already facing
    insurmountable odds . . .
tricky dicks,
    disreputable scumbags
foul balls on three & two counts
submarines in the marsh, tanklessness
    can't stop runaway trains, double-deckers
tremens, legends, rugs in the yard
    a 2× loser in a lineup
I repeat myself
    but I wish I was a better writer

maybe then
    I could convince someone
    w/ powers that be . . .
that this is what I should be doing
    4th 1/4, last ditch effort
    game on the line . . .
that's why I'm carrying it—too far
upon a × once again

OPPOSITES ATTRACT

artichokes & vast conspiracies
    of what you can & cannot do
    of death and ignominy
what the wind's about
    about gunpowder & firecrackers
don't do it
    said the monkey to the jackanapes
    . . . glue to a horse
common sense and tired flesh
    worms & moss . . .
fatima, lourdes, guadaloupe
teatime for whales,
    make peace w/ past wrongs
genocide is much more than an indiscretion
nobody wins in a war,
    he who created whores & pimps
    she was a nuclear disaster
transcendence reincarnated
    naked on a beach
    bent nails & tilted crosses

a blip on the radar,
    while you were blinking,
    we passed off the passé
and built a statue in the park
    the grounds became sacrosanct
    the king was dead
long live the queen

I'M AN ACTRESS, NOT A HOOKER!!!

poppycock & putrification
I swallowed the pills they gave me
75 acres to race with
    arm wrestling female ninjas
the hunters exiting
the storm of angels
    w/ swollen wings
closure of the armageddon
    and starving children in the hills
it's co-oold outside . . .
    bells wrung on st. crispin's day
good morning professors,
    officers, little school girls
go speed racer,
    he's a demon, and he's coming after someone
    she's a whore & that's all there is to it
the smell of asparagus & roses

the traffickers of amexica, teheran, ohio
  sex, drugs & sayonara . . . konichiwa
  jaws of the new ice age . . . immortality
enamorata in single file
  I don't speak punjabi
carry on dearth of inklings
  somebody swab the decks quickly
pappy was a crappy salesman
  anyhow, it is what it is!

WHY . . . THE NERVE
OF SOME . . . !

localized with introductions
    checking electrolytes w/ anomalies
in the wake of a sea shanty
    scars & extinguishers, guitars & accordions
a swill of celebrity
a news broadcast,
    beneath the sea of enchantment
    behind the cold war, iron curtain
sex wax in the butter arcade
    turbocharged sales pitch, compounded interests of
scallywags & rapscallions
    the french foreign legionnaires
    thirsty for answers
jury duty, stock analysis, commissary funds
    we played checkers in siberia
I capitalized on missing links
    the connectivity of alien genetics

drop a camera on a meteorite

sin and sin again

    the narcissisms of incarcerations

a mafia tailspin, corkscrewing

a product in a costumization

    we make the best of microwaves & the internet

text, text . . . pull &

    anger mgt. is a neuroscience

when hell is what we live in . . .

& heaven is what we try to make of it

WHY I DON'T GIVE A HOOT

background check?
    you should have seen me coming
    the shit on my shoes, my country 'tis pour moi
before you made me
              a corporate sponsor of
a planned obsolescence owlation
    and conspicuous consumption
sociopathy, psychotherapy, pathology
    hijacked in gym class, on the run
    corpse on a morgue slab abs
    pit bull of a stage mom, distant dad & dysfunctional family
pre-pubescent alchoholism
drug addled behaviorialisms, insecurity
    insider trading of paradoxicals
 extremism, proclivities amuck
    the power of pop, famousness, triviality
    and other lowest common denominators

yo-yo-yoisms, mr. and mrs. happening
    and other interchangeable commodities
putting mufflers on the merrymakers in tandem
    w/ a successful receivership
    of incorporated madnesses
annoying paparazzi, tits & ass
    who make livings off of us & uses of,
    other proactive innuendoes
that comes up as popularity on TV, etc.
tweeting & twerking
with vacuous ennui

WHEN I'M NOT WORTHY
OF ALL THE TIME

strolling on a golf course
    I ain't never played—the links, the greens a grain of sand
the stream of rain
       turns into a river
she wears a low-cut dress
    I'm not all that interested
she's been with too many men
     understand, I'm being honest
sometimes life just seems unbearable
seeing the forest & its ghosts, traps, wholes
    for the trees, birch to sassafras,
watching purposelessly,
    as the dead die around the world
I'm no angel
    and I hope I can admit when I'm wrong
thank god,
    I never had to kill anyone

I know I'm capable of it
but, I want to get out of here, this × around
    thank god for small blessings
    & hissy scratches on film
it makes me think of bigger things
    like tennis anyone???
     like fini & c'est kaput
la petite morte, and storming the bastille
    great events I had little to do with
so this stuck btw. the rock & the proverbial
hard places, where I had × to write poems,
that might be of more worth
    than this, that, or me

RECOGNIZE

it's whitey, our gang, this ol' town
    other dead end kids from the streets
gun battle, knife fight, bare knuckles
    knock some sense into thick skulls, open eyes
greasy hangouts, slutty women
    earn a living on your back, or standing tall
big pimping, bacon bits, picket fence
    shitty eyebrows, learning french
the noir and henpeck
    swinging from the candelabra
on with the show!!!
    even if it's hard to fit it all in @ once
leaving on a jet plane
left out in the cold, set on fire
    outclassed in the outback
doing kung fu on an elephant's back
    rattling guns of sycophants
the doctor's couch is no place to rest up
then change your bandages, once a day, baby
    you're too damaged to go on

trust funds, off-shore banking business
the vestiges of the crumbling empire
    what goes up must come down
irrefutable laws of thermo-nuclear dynamics
    for every action . . . an equal
    and opposite re-action always comes
that's why we keep on keeping on
& thank your lucky stars, you got to see @ least one

OFF THE BENCH

old hills, cold coffee, relief pitcher
    nothing left to do but pull in peaches
swab decks,
    stand up spinning
duck questions,
    wonder why royalties never amounted to much
common wonder,
    even though I wore ties to catholic school
    everyday for twelve years
phase shifter, electron capacitator
    beam me up scottie, I need new weapons
I've fallen down stairs
it got crowded amongst the stars
I'm pitching from the stretch position
    still playing hardball w/ a bunch of fags
this pack of cigarettes
the said overload of useless information
    still waters run deep
but nobody
    wants to hear what somebody else has to say

pay to play,
one way or the other
housewife, attorney,
    #6 on the all-× major league hits list
I didn't even come close
it must be true,
    I spent my life in the negative zone
and even superman had no interest in saving me

FITTING IN

billiards, aerobics, kick the can
    you got a pastime, blond ambition
    don't matter to anybody else in the world
I won't give up
    till my blood flows into the Yangtze River
car parts & mullets
celebrity fist fucking
    fishheads in soup, stir & serve
as if,
    crack was a missing ingredient
guam was the center
      of the urdu speaking peoples
put your french on the table
    change shortstops, excuse punctuation
newspapers, flights, horses
    the daily of certain activities
    that certain species have in common
I'm certain
I'd lay my eyeballs on it
    or, is it, the triangulation of pyramids

refiguration, youthful speculation

    god was in love once too

just like I was

    the 1st × & thought I

    knew exactly what I was doing

historically representative

of square pegs & round holes

PERHAPS

narcopan and nunchuks
    dudes of clockwise confessions
super pretzels, plantains, meekrob
    if the shoe fits, wear the hat
the crow, who became army scouts
the actor, who portrayed a mafia boss
    a doctor to the pharaoh approaching
sometimes, it's even too hard, too silly
    to clearly understand, the simple truth
words are like sugar candy worms
    70,000 carloads of trains
    overused, outdated & full of fracked gas & tips
danger, will robinson
    what do you mean we, kimosabe!
newspaper to eat,
    for the poor & hungry, diseased & lonely
to the polls
    ye sons of freedom & chastisement
nude perspectives of dead assassins
sexy anger of out of work monarchists

the corporate control of royalties
a burden of sin and confusion,
    how to twiddle thumbs!
the ground erupts w/ further cryptics
the skies are full of new war
    and creepy genetics, organized to perform
better than my ideas of . . .
theft & solace ever could've

LEMONADE CHOICES

shrimp in a bottle
    changing reflections
    acting the superior, tits ahoy
an army on its belly
    crawling the universe
three-legged dogs
    who warm all the spellings
descriptive, non-denominational, secularized
    flowers of eden, nirvana, elysium
halcyon days, lightbulb ideas, steamrollers
    the shooting gallery spins
    contracts in a graveyard
the corrupt steroids of youth, school, marriage
the balance you were wounded with
    nothing left but the vampires & fishmongers
you lie with enjoyment environs
    the new fix, the missing shits
compress, stints, silhouettes
    bring up the ammunition
more filthy bandages & corpse medals

    seadog minions,
huns on horses, gooks in trees
snowflakes, grubstakes, extinction
species & their animal indifferences
    the choosers & their chosen ones
    this kingdom heaven
@ the bottom of the wishing well
becomes bubblegum

THE WHISPERS
OF SAMEHDI

the news of cows,
    calliopes & kaleidoscopes
the magic lantern turns
    sidecar to a general election
we rode away . . .
    amidst the shouts of hey!!!
    . . . and what the fuck???
there's no accounting,
    of others' foreign sensibilities
silkworm and sluicegate
    what comes down the pike
slash & burn, born special, interrogations
    the guts to fight the system
    this devil's playground
        . . . not since superman
hawkeye, sgt rock, pilgrim . . . & blackbeard
    round again, beneath the wheel

the karma, darma, fait accompli
     . . . soldier in the rain
the one that got away
   from the plans of mice & men
we slept in rows of burnt out occupants
   & put our pants on once a day
the crunchy, melting, wishy-washy
the broken glass, the apropos & teriyaki
   gitchee, goomie, st. germaine
the waterfall we all must see through
the sorrow of the horses in the mines

WHAT CAN WE SAY?

we write epitaphs
   quoting saints, sinners, self-help gurus & Japanese poets
waiting for the other foot to fall
   templars, friars, rosicrucians, jesuits of consternation
as we walk across
   the burning sands
   the peaks of mountain tops
   this borrowed sense of independence
a luncheon of parishioners,
   in front of the board of stockholders
9 to 5, march in ×, tall timbers, all is well
   chop-chop, or you'll take all day
   campers, delinquents, prophets, shiksa
   capitals & monograms, stateside envoy
all ashore,
   w/ these last minute details
remember, you can't throw good after bad
   luck of the draw, previous engagement
we cowards die 1,000 ×s a day
what it was, how you got there

I saw what god did
and understand you as well
cheap synthetics just don't cut it
we said enough already
the toilet overflows
commandments, tablets & papal bulls
it's what goes down, off this coil
and around a block of granite

HAPPY DON'T WORRY . . . ?

out of work worry worts . . . & ghosts of . . .
 special forces, union bosses
 cardinals, orioles & blue jays
alimony and extreme unctions
a trust fund, in the newsroom,
  a self-medicated backlog
isolation in space
 don't throw tomatoes, all @ the same ×
my '50's mentality
 bullies from god, firecrackers, 45s
 drinking in McSorley's
 driven over the bridge, in stolen cars
I've got away w/ everything but murder
 it made me 1/2 a criminal
don't exponentialate the exascervations
 1984, the sleepy guards, dank trickeries
 you still
 gotta pick me up f/ work in the AM, yes sir, Ø sir
 50% toll increases, inflation rise
conflict of interests, cronyisms, paranoia

if no one hears the whistle blowing
do bears shit in the woods? on Sun.?
decapitated customers, industrial explosions
decrepit infrastructures in superstorm upgrade
you need to put up the best you got
conspiracies be thy name, whatevers
systemic injustices in an overwhelming lack of interest
. . . happy

STILL GOT
A WAYS TO GO

alone in the living room
    I write like space was colliding w/ infrastructure
eyeballs spin, nose flares
    sugarland, backwater, sky train, hellavator
and all the inbetween countryside & bothersome
cut your losses, walk on by
    let the hammer fall . . .
stick a screwdriver in the ceiling
    fix the blinds, the sink, the latest bugaboo
wallpaper chic,
    tailwinds of suicide
you just come back here again as fit punishment
    till you learn how to do it right!
transference of energy
translucent to iridescent
    baby, got lightbulbs, 3-way to 100 wattage
tacks on the carpet, rug worn, throw down

art deco, farmers market, burial plot
didn't think the road less traveled
    would end up being diabetic w/ false promises
static electricity
the cling of karma will never die
    the heavens of all your tomorrows
where you still gotta, hernias or not,
    pick your feet up & put 'em down
cracked sidewalk, tilted slope, doors to floors
    how we get from 1 end of
our existence to the other, w/o stepping out on our own!

BEAUTIFUL BANDAGES

flirtation's anatomy, justifiable homicides
    wallflower, cock of the walk, don't be a dud
when the party's over, who pays
what songs were sung off key in the shower,
    balladeer, doo-wop, torchier, belted bowtie
she was shown a dead girl baby
    that belonged to another mother's other drama
baskets in the reeds
    a raft downriver slowly
    a debt of demonized like any such luck, as
my religion became a hospital bill
    your voice, as louder now
sweating marbles, lifting feathers
    betting on the benefit of the doubt
in good faith, 2 states away, on foreign soil
goodwill hunt, promises of the education
    and what you could've done on your own
    if you'd been left alone to do your job
my work phasing
    edifications in repose

don't aggravate my pulses

42 days till the past fits into place

there's always 30 blanks to fill

bullets should've flown by now

out back, in the back of the head

now I lay me down, but couldn't sleep

till I found my wallet empty game

and figured out who was taking out the garbage

DANGER BREWING

blanched canaries
    the dope on Poughkeepsie, Canarsie, Donetsk
    the newspaper read, front to back
why we shouldn't miss obituaries...
    the call to arms of beckoning fingers
    the dilly dally talliwackers bent
breathe deep . . . the simulated reality
    and paid downs on certain debts & futures
working w/ interior tools,
    and special interests, paid lobbyists,
       of party politics & disinformation
wishes of never listening
    I know you're coming in the morning
    so I can hurry up, and die
or, should I,
    just angrier than the average bear
dog breath, angel hair, paw tattoo
    buenos aires, lima, mexico city
cops, they're never aroind when you need them
    hanoi, jakarta, sydney, nuclear tsunami

your kung fu is not good enough... mate
    looks like I'm going to have to publish
heaven & hell itself
    designer kills, psychiatric burdens
an oology of making painted, furry, fuzzy
on the planet of dysfunctional species
      endangered perspectives,
mating rituals, and specific warnings about said conditions

DESERT CROSSING

witchcraft & trinkets, windblown kisses
   the ersatz medieval system
recouperage & lipstick taxes
   an empty house of women's problems
mickey mouse @ the oasis in college & pantomime
   donald duck wears a sombrero
on to the guillotine, vive la revolution
   time for frogs & franks & beans
salsa w/ candelabra, tostados & tortillas
   a latticework of lace & snakeskin
   a terrify, speechy, la luna eclipses
swoll CIA, DEA, snakeheads, spetznats
   ice picks to a trotsky in place once upon a worldwide ×
   easy to the yokohama mamas
   radioactive sicarios of unilateral force
bring baseball back with enhancements
   . . . queridas??? . . . drugs & nafta
   maquiladores, mandalas de la sambras
Tijuana, Juarez & Laredo (coast, gulf & border)
   motorcycles & the I-35 corridor to Duluth, Minn.

Sinaloa, Mixtec, Zetas, all the Amexica motherfuckers
    coyote=wolfman, frankenstein to super soldier
    dracula, walking dead, zombie & bruja
    headless corpses hung as messages
hood & scythe oaths to santissimo muerte, el guiso
the hurly burly, mish-mash, mucho macho
the modern trafficante & its pursuant
corruptions . . . plata o ploma, a vat of narcopowders
& mix in the creepy crawlies

PREDICTABLE #S

the whosoe'er firstborn
   of misdirected irony
a chastisement of defeat
an agony of crawling forth
   this extremonious superfluosity
gears & cogs, erector sets, duct tape
   the approaching cosmicornucopia
   the advance into the clarion haloid
spiderwise, incestivoid, beeswax, etc.
   obliviously misunderstood taxation
   to volatile consternation
judas' sin was one of despair, Ø betrayal
   kneeling in the garden crying, weepy
before the cock crows twice
   you will deny me thrice
this wholesale as retribution
the perambulisms of motivation's materialism
   square & compass, fifth dimension
   surfside, starquest, 666, the # of the beast

the physical planet permutations

    a 7th rung to heaven, marriage purple nirvana

the ∞ infirmity of situational being ad infinitum

the 9th planet,

the key to universal ending, finito pluto

the old in out, duo-decimal, tenfold

energy is neither created nor destroyed,

    no one gets out of here alive anyway

OFFICIAL ENDS

8 ball in the corner pocket
    don't scratch the cue
don't knock yourself out trying to win
    play the %s of wow,
    easier said than done
homework, overtime, anger mgt.
    the cost of earning a living
say your prayers . . . about when
    maybe, you'll become a professional
    @ what you do best
balance the budget
    therapeutics, gymnastics, dietetics
    tried & found wanting in the past
armed adversaries, bombing & airstrikes
    history follows patterns
    repeating itself, when ill advised
    surges and counterpoints
this threat of citizenship, more than
    living right next door to an angel
open classrooms of visionary tactics

fountain of youth, scrap metal
gushy mush, jumping the gun, reconfigurations
giving up the non-objective
    prison camps, combat units, black ops
gross national products
    of non-denominational secularisms
    of fried onions & bread baskets
and the doctor said, "have you got an appointment???"

THAT FEELING
OF SLIM PICKINGS

a diet of lettuce & worms
an area of expertise
a suffragette's caborring
      between 2 cities
the finger lake district, 1,000 rivers
the history of ides
you can make a cartoon out of me
an @ your leave, between appts.
axle grease, bitten reins, ox breath
a sudden disappearance,
      of the dinosaur
pterodactyl, brontosaurus
   stegosaurus, tyrannosaurus rex
the dope amongst brothers
the stopover of politicism
   when movies end on time
an advantage has been taken

where not enough were given
society of wherewithals
a long wind in the mountains
a full call of the wild
pastoral, bucolic, picturesque
... tree spirited
the cost of letting go
the pride of true existentialists
the storied exchange
and a lack of anything further to be said

TAGS OF SPOKEN GLORY

it's just that lemmings clientele
       milk is spooky
take me back to woodstock
take me to your leader
take the time to know you, mucho caliente
          one step beyond
the infamous inspector 7
the last one in the pool
w/o sergio, I hope your pants Ø fit
driving a tractor on a drug farm
   in this dingy little backwater of a town
if you don't see the cock go in the pussy
   you can't talk about it
bring me the head, body bags
   of all those concerned
black mail, plagiarism, homage
   why you wanna do a brother like that
the proof is in the truth
turning jeffersons into lincolns
to walk alone, a blister on the sun

what if you lived in Harrisburg, or
were a rice paddy daddy
    a victim of environment
    a she-demon, fuck the system
beer is good, but pussy is great, sex w/ sheep
life sucks, kill yourself . . . bring it
but don't come under here, I got a gun under here

THE CREATIVE CRIMINALITY

repellant recidivism, conjunctivitis
   welt, spindle, fold
corrective insurance dating
   get me to the church on time
baptism of fire, cold potato soup
back up against the wall
   a lapse in the terrorism, a uniformality
 sky high explosions
   of petty exuberance
shoppers' delight, tasked to performance
   crows deliver babies
   chariot races of drugged slaves
tarzan is in the trees again
   knife fight in an exercise yard
sweet good-byes to locusts & cigarettes
   kisses in doorways, on subway platforms
   on boat docks across the world
yankee doodle macaroni
   fasten seatbelts please
handheld action, sped up focus

naked figures in the wash
cuckold w/ a firearm
in technicolor revolution
rhumba, conga, mambo
fly me to the moon in chains
the shame of mating w/ a
subspecies
quiet on the set, I'm still composing

A COHERSIVE ESPIONAGE

knee deep in the smoke
    soldiers in uniform, policia,
eagle's nest, shrimp boat, bamboo forest
    blackmarket high command
barbed wire around the kick, drumbeat clockwise
waltzing w/ the particulars
    an orchestrated ingenious
venison, partisans, a pastiche of tactics
     as she ascended staircases
    beauty moved in mysterious ways
rocks on train tracks
    the horseshit mistaken for
spear of destiny, holy grail, goombahs
    eyebrows under visors squinting
 viper in the grass slithers
    agents stuck in spaceships
the retribution of sideways
the illegitimacy of business
    séance in the afternoon
dredging the canal

for matching pearl-handled pistols
who's the shooter???
lingering criminal conspiracies
OSS, G-2, P-2, CIA, FBI, DEA, Interpol
an international pie eating contest
in a gross obesity action
thin waisted, trim gams, nice rack of pussé on the side
and murder on the highway

SENSING MAGNESIUM

pearls before swine, alien instructions
  eggs over easy, tight fits
the pyramids' design
  shafts of light
a year in Lisbon, sensing change
  studying architecture
these graphic novels
  are bottling mayhem
maintaining relations
  is harder than it looks
a reflective legacy
  in the hands of a confederacy of dunces
the streets roll out
  as we begin to understand existence
I feel as if
  the ink is lifting off the pages
bandages become undone
    I bought a car, went to war
and ran out of everything . . . inalienable rights
money, gas, energy, lies, emotions

the tired bent of even . . . shadows
    all the tricks of a magician
prestidigitations, manifestations, heroics
    the chemicals of the periodic table
    the pope's blessing & prayers
    the wishes of my fellow human beings
all the news that's fit to print
and any other suitable forms of alternative secret identities

FRUSTRATION'S CHOWTIME

obnoxious bellowings
   the sound of movement on the road
   travails in a box, strewn tools, swollen eye
a joker's cowardice,
      cloudy mistakes
cirrus, cumulous, nimbus
   a quarterback's hail mary
the jets better keep matt simms
   and you know I don't like to call out
special names, or a series of plays
   chords & notes, mr. melody . . . only tempo
everyone in a league of their own
      a separate voice
waterfront commission, mob affiliation,
      longshoremen's union
why can't we all just get along???
   superstorms, bermuda triangle, deluges
hot tar on your bare back,
      feel the damn heat
coke & pepsi, heroin & its derivative opiates

privatized consumptions
promo code dial-ins
the noir of social media as . . .
planned obsolescence
kibbutz & collective
a clan of the armed & aggravated
w/ a strikeout of the sides
bored w/ dominoes & pizza for lunch

CATCH THESE CRIMINALS

it's raining all over china
I'm confused by all the commercials
    only the dead can flog the dying
indian fighters, sepoys, pirates
    the wars convene w/ time
knife in the belly, mud by the hut
    a sheriff's badge, a zulu shield
the arrow's flight
the shot & fodder,
    lying down in the fields of the lord
johnny got a gun,
    but refused to join the arab uprising
the ukraine is not part of russia, period
the death squads of right-wing military dictatorships
they're all still guilty, the sorry mighty
    of being mass murderers, kill, kill . . .
and almost only counts
    in horseshoes & hand grenades
violence is still a matter of intent
    turned cheek, etc., thrice before thrice

all ideals,

 crammed & stuffed into one-line solipsisms

body bags,

 and saying worried in court

mea culpa, mea culpa

 camouflage vs. taupe

arm in a sling, a suited uniform to form

WHILE WARS
ARE BEING FOUGHT

I see paris on the corner
    flat oceans, cold pears
skyscrapers along the tree line
    to do a 1st class work of art
    we have to know how to do the right thing
cultural evidences,
    bas-relief, corinthian leather
the fragilities of social structures
    dead members of one's own family
cross dimensionals throughout the museum
    the weight of subject matter
the consequence of involving depths
the smell of corrupted flesh
the alone of standing in the wings
the delay of decades, centuries, lifetimes
    a cameo in a boring movie
salvages of a garbage dump

a long scow into the darkness sails
faith as an allegorical theory
    an america full of aliens, armies
    and inalienable draperies
the kitchen full of philippinos, jews & sins
the commissions of the rich
the sources of the nile, milk, ghosts, gum
the slavery of concepts
the millions of great states of state
    we friends of artists & geniuses
who became sainted by the extent of their deeds

DRAWN IN WITH

renewed vows of celebrity status
    we the public relativities & itises
the spectacles of science
the watching of me & you
    but on different elevators, planets
you advised me to remain silent
    that I was being too cryptic
    the nasty, most, reality plus
    the housing of elves & poor dwarves with no tussin
    the legends all die
most warranted w/o inspections
    don't empty the pool just yet
    don't rake the leaves w/o a season
the ink ain't dry . . . how to cut facts
    × bites your tattoos
it's receivables as documentations
    grandma's dirty drinks
the ravenous raw
the ugly specifics
    a publicity of idiosyncrasies

an ugly uglier still lives
I busted a union
took pictures of its officials
bribed all the usuals
and took interest in lobbyists
as proof of sleeping with the enemy
and awoke married to a discussion

INSPIRATIONAL IMPROVISATION

let jesus be your gang leader (f/ cry baby)
john the baptist
        was selling holy water
bathe in profits,
        wear headphones on 1 ear
see you in hell . . . angel face, baby doll
        blondie brick road, taps &
hub caps, cheater slicks, upholstery
    the devil's head through a hole in the ground
rockin' & rollin', going,
        round & round . . . 360°
diamond chiselers, counterfeit greenbacks
        sing your ever lovin' heart out
we met on a Sun.
we were buried on a Friday next
        Sat. was a trainwreck
hullabaloo, shindig, freak-out

cyclone & tunnel of love
wormholes in your empty head
the joint, the hoosegow, the slammer
somebody's always doing time
a blind date w/ an unfit companion
doctor, lawyer, Indian chief
it's hard to be specific, sergeant
when you're hunting the great white whale
w/ taxes on a stand up bass & stolen beats
I'm from hunger, a raging lamo
while the stars @ ngt. provide
the heat blast as well as the electricity

THEY HID HITLER'S
COCKAMAMIE
(I ONLY HID MY OWN)

I'm in the jailhouse now,
   god bless my probation officer
naked on the golf course, in a downtown office
   robbing parking meters for quarters
oversized military uniforms
an elongated paper trail
   no credits in the roll-up
the bunny hops in town, the catholic guilt of the '50s
   newspapers full of tramps & hussies
there's a wussie on the telephone
   I remember those who die young
we made license plates, sweaters, did laundry
   ran the mile more than once
   played wiffle ball in summer yards
stole cars & went over the GWB @ midnight

did garage rock in the super's basement
al the knife played a hollowbody
          black ovation
there's a big beak in our business
     heroin buried in a goombah's lawn
mau mau racing across the Belgian Congo
     gunshots heard outside Dunkin' Donuts
Jacko & las chicas
     almost made it to Tito Puente's gig
          later . . . for the ½ a criminals
when the rats & bed bugs
     of post WWII & the holocaust
got away w/ genocides and fled U.S. intelligence, Vatican bankroll
     swiss guard w/ Jewish gold, into Sth. Amer. hideways

AS IF IT WERE
WRITTEN ON THE WALL

old age crept up on me,
     like a thief in the liars club
subverted any sense of justice
     that I had left
blue angels, red devils, whiskey hot heat
   a balance in the wash & rehab
seascapes, barnyard fowl, tits ahoy,
      chinese checkers
your timing's good in the rain & thunder
you've kept your ownership, partners
      of Rome on fire
winterscapes, superstorms, armeggedons
   c'mon in supersuckers & tyrants
endangered species, airstrike convoys
   come over red rover, pigeons, plovers
creature did, the supercilious
   a hung man's hard-on pissing down his leg

cards on the table, aces & 8s
    the dynamo is humming
the picards, turpitudes, responsibilities
stop the world, I want to get off
    clean & reorganized morality
the job is mine, if I want it!
    batman, aquaman, green arrow
a blackhawk of eminent domain
as if one could manage on one's own
    w/o god's help???, sincerely
I doubt it!

ALL-SENSING

it ain't easy
    coloring books, paint by #s, plagiarism
living under the meloik
    queens over jacks, working in the mines,
        thor's hammer blows
being a waitress, wearing sneakers
    & clothes made of cowhide, cotton, or canvas
sleeping on mars,
    bent pillows & crying bandages
the ugliest dream murmurs
the blood dissipates
    in the war-torn valleys
diseases come looking,
    some came running
in the wake of clouds
in between the churning islands
    @ ×s there're only pincers
needles, scissors, gauze & cling
    an ironing board in the kitchen
pots on the walls

and ink that won't dry
plainer to see the nose on an enemy's
    taciturn & succinct face
    w/ insects for eyes
crawling, creeping, climbing closer
burning images into facts
but I guess there's a place for all god's bits & pieces
    in the world of universal dimensions

THEATRICAL DRAPERY

a policy to uphold
    precedential & obligatorily
even in an intemperate climate
    warm ice, cold, strength,
        a glass eye
a necklace of teeth
a welcoming death
an animal's capitulation
    to surrounding circumstances
inevitable dramatics & dialogue,
    a fury of conscience,
what's more the rebel???
    unfortunate, the quiet terms
    of involuntary response
wrestling vistas & entanglements
    upper hands & lower unmentionables
whispering riddles
    in desperation on placards
the intensity of mystifications
then hold all the enmity possible

don't put too much importance
on de-classifications
the ayes have it, in megabytes
in the belly of the beast
the definition found by this, an agency
the lawyer in the library,
a motion to standards
scared & magnetized by . . . set direction

ANY SONG W/ THE WORD BABY IN IT CAN'T BE ALL BAD

passport to the stars,
    a kid's gotta dream, don't she
long drives, visiting parent planet
    panic in a war-torn world
and I know
    somewhere out there
there's a barrel full of monkeys
    and they're all laughing at me
    holding severed heads, wagging their tongues
playing parcheesi, monopoly, bingo
    melting butter over low flames
    making paper-mâché, masks
and whispering about next year's mardi gras . . . ,
    down there in the smoke,
demons speak our names

we concentration-camp victims
we who seek not martyrdom, nor sainthood
but a just us,
in a workable habitat & salary cap
the dentist's bill for grillwork
the taxi transport to the end of the dock
the high-flying trapeze & breakdown
the baby's ba, at sprinkled temperature
read to your offspring
even if they're sleeping,
they'll hear the sound of your voice
be-ubba-bubba-bicky-bye-b, b, b, b-aby

ADVANCEMENT

. . . charge!!!
   the cavalry's coming
the arrows are flying
   raining, teardrops, & 2ℂ pencils
every work of art, or,
   attempt thereforth
has at least some redeeming value
   a peace offering to the large ogres & giants of industry
time is on... my side
   Van Gogh's ear of offended sensibility
cut from a whore's purse
   in pursuit of a separate peace
   and a contemporary's maceable action
chump change, and talent scouts
   we offered you cash on the barrelhead
for your deeds of valor, princely honor
   and your international copyrights
intellectuals be damned,
   there're catapults & trebuchets
set up outside,

the moat & drawbridge of the castle
my kingdom, for a horse
 a saddle & a six shooter
 a flame of calcutta & religious freedom
 a lawgiver @ the parapets
 a bowel movement in prison
when the levee's broken,
something's gotta give . . .

WHAT TO DO
WITH THE DEAD
AND DYING

bandits, pirates, soothsayers
    prettier heads have fallen
take your brutish ass on out of here
the colonies, protectorates, subsidiaries
the nature of the stock exchange . . . of goods
    I gamble with your life!!!
our emphasis is on the paraphrased idiomatic
    someday, we'll all be friends
l'amore, slàinte, muons f/ space
    what a good craig we could've had
probabilities most likely,
posterity won't have you, or your bag of coins
    nights away from home
a stolen base in the 9th inning ties the game
    shearing the winds of time

all basic knowledge,
    but a contract & commitment
psoriasis @ the end of the day
    the snake will shed its skin
    but still must crawl the earth
    clinging to the sphere of physical pain
you gotta dime, I need to make a call
    buy an extra set of legs . . . , # of days
so I can walk off in the distance
    take this scam for a ride
build tanks & planes, aircraft carriers
    make a foreign sovereignty
and bury your ass . . . dust to dust, radioactivity

WHY TALK ABOUT IT?

dutch east india trading company
    suck-cess in the sugarcane
the slaves who died went overboard
    during the middle passage
jump down & pick a bale of cotton
    build a railroad, transcontinental
supercalifragilisticexpialidocious
    the true name of yahweh
    the drug cartels of super highways
    there's an out of control fire
in the backrooms of justice
    put on a pressed shirt
even though you decry life's calamities
don't let anyone know
    what a train wreck you really are
even though you'll probably never walk normal again,
    let them know, your hands . . .
can still scrawl, and
    let no other write your epitaph
graveyard, headstone, youthful prayers,

evidence of extreme unction
only, roasted potatoes,
    and statistics that bind
genetic mutations, parables, crosses
    nails & dirt, crops & seeds
what you owe . . . because life is debt
make no doubt about it,
even if it's perceived as rewritten history

BETWEEN OASES,
TIME & CONSCIOUSNESS

gruesome consequences
    to ignorance & its self-serving bliss
echoes in the abyss, chasms, valley
      the slow-moving vehicle coming up
      the trail, ravine, moraine
stock analysis, inverted lawsuits
some, whose to blame,
         for all of us
floaters, as far as the eye can see
    daylight in the swamp
    an independence f/ former colonies
satrap, mullah, viceroy
    canaries who will spend their lives in a cage
bamboo, eggshell, gilded
    prostrated before kings, imams, emperors
I think therefore I am . . . the slave
    of intelligence, compulsion, the corporation

rights & laws of fundamentalisms
      fireproof, prodigals, parameters
I thought of circumference/diameter/radii
      a postmortem on a bird of paradise
I was reading up on . . .
      about the increased cost of plane flights
      panhandlers & freeloaders
            w/ angels, wings & haloes
      oxidizers & fertilizers in oxygenated stir
            tanks in an army
coming to an island in the stream

A CAGE W/ WINDOWS

she brought a bird to the birdman
    a car to the mechanic
    a sad soul to the music
widowmaker, oil rigging, warden's pardon
      the sound of beauty w/ a smile
      the threat of power
convictions of publicity
   neck & neck w/ old law books
   in the face of pharmaceutical lobbyists
   drop platform of a hanging judge
I just can't lie fast enough
   you'll understand less & less
but it'll never be $\leq$,
      the both of us
lot & his wives,
   angels & their dreams of translucence
some worms that really dig in
   right on brothers & sisters
pop, the revolution's coming
dear sirs, the computerized end of this

    shit you've been flouting f/ years
obstruction of justice,
    of anything that gets in your underwear
lice, fleas, profit sharing
    bolshevism, socialists, unionism
can't con an old con
can't bullshit a bullshitter
and that's why they're all about it

COITUS INTERRUPTUS

jackhammer to desertion
   the young eat their dead
   the illusions of daily life
   the consciousness of awakened memory
buy me a microscope
   because I can't see anymore
pastels & cork, the darting heritage
   one-liners can get you flattery
   but won't buy you a retirement plan
I.O.U's, copywritten forms, IRA's, IQ
   the pathology of geniuses
   the dollar's slide, the B-movie star career
you demanded more ice,
   I couldn't make it hot enough
to care about what you're doing
   as a sort of personal responsibility
King David's psalm,
     Sheba's cloven foot trek
the fracking results to groundwaters
the research of aids & ebola drugs

how to farm the population of Mexico
and any other adjacent
    isthmus, peninsula, fiord, space station
the quickest line between two points
    north star, southern equinox, east of the wall
we still gotta age before the camera
    meet w/ the parole board, clock w/ the
projectories, marry the one who loves us & procreate

PARAPHRASED INTO SUBMISSION

you—you!!!
    me tarzan, who walk alone
a page in the directory
a salvage job, from the dumps . . .
    my finished product
    mostly written in the dark
don't let life be taken from her @ any cost
    my daughterism by any other name
    my suzie cream cheese, enforced consignee, purple nirvana
I wasn't in it alone,
    my tough as nails ex- . . . wife
I did try to make you happy . . .
    guess it wasn't in my providence
old thief, trustee respect, gourmet grab-ass
once queen of denial, likely on auto-pilot,
    bull in a china-shop
    surrounded by the rest of the eggiweggs

this savage languination,
    sanguineria, portals, bitters
habilis, to invest again w/ dignity
    Ø the recidivism & denatured euphemism
remember rule #15
    of the no good motherfucker handbook
you know you're a scumbag
    when your wife shoots you in the stomach
@ least it didn't come to that
and thus, that doesn't mean that we can't take a joke

LEFTOVERS TO DELIVER

the cosmic clown force on a stolen page
the dogs of war, sins of man, lockdown
the breaking up is hard to do,
     3 the hard way, 7 come 11
jacob's ladder, pseudopsychiatrics
     surrender your arms
peter pan, shoemaker, atom bomb,
     the naked & the dead
@ least, you never lied to me, right dracula
     blood sucker, living dead, scorpion's sting
only because, the other foot hasn't dropped yet,
I know it's coming,
     only because I also know
CBGB's, the Court Tavern & the Brighton all closed
     but the hunger hasn't subsided
     and I still haven't gotten my due
pay scale, books published, recording contract
     signed, sealed, & delivered
does the world owe you a living
     of course it does, of course it does

norma jean, eugene debs, name dropping pillow talk
 god's chosen few, I am one of those
indian madmen, prophet & soothsayer
 re-iterating catchphrases, swift charm
jedi knight, corny toad, turtle on log, slim jim
 knight rider till the break of dawn
gun shot on the floor
nothing left to give but the price of eggs & the time of day

ABOUT THE AUTHOR

Jacko Monahan was born in Passaic, N.J., and grew up on the streets of Palisades Park. During the 1980s, he was the front man and lyricist for the punk rock/hard core bands Fatal Rage and Dirge. Fatal Rage put out a single eponymous LP in 1983, but the latter band released numerous recordings, including two LPs—*Flesh Crawler* and *Soul Storm.* Having begun his musical career as a teenager in Palisades Park, Monahan has worked in some forty different bands in a variety of genres, writing original lyrics for them all, and has appeared on at least thirteen recordings.

He also served for twenty-three years as the booking agent at the Brighton Bar, an original music venue in Long Branch, N.J. He estimates that he put on 10,000 shows at the Brighton and other venues, such as The Saint and The Stone Pony in Asbury Park and The Court Tavern in New Brunswick. Among these shows were the monthly poetry readings at the Brighton Bar.

Monahan started writing poetry when he was fifteen and has continued to produce poems at a prodigious rate ever since. "I had a fascination with words from an early age," he says. His work has appeared in *Wanderlust, This Broken Shore,* and *The Idiom.* A number of his poems appeared recently in *Palisades, Parkways & Pinelands: An Anthology of Contemporary Poets* (Blast Press, 2015).

ABOUT THE PUBLISHER

Meet Me in Botswana:
What is **BLAST PRESS?**

A speech for national poetry month about BLAST PRESS by Gregg Glory

Ab li dolen in l'air

[look up: beauty falls from the air]

"A book should be a ball of light in your hands."
~~ Ezra Pound

As we all know, April is "International Guitar Month." But my heart twangs for poetry, and I was invited here to tell you a little bit about a tiny poetry publishing company called **BLAST PRESS**.

Let's start with what **BLAST PRESS** is not. **BLAST PRESS** is not a community. It is not a community-building venture. It is not by, about, or for "the people." Unlike the pretentious anthologies that weigh down university shelves and slander the individual by gluing him into some historian's scripted story, **BLAST PRESS** is not a collection of individual voices expressing the vibrancy, meaning, and tradition of the creative community—nor of any community. In this respect, **BLAST PRESS**, as its critics have bitterly asserted, is nothing at all.

BLAST PRESS has published over 100 chapbooks and softbacks by some thirty authors over the past quarter century. Each author's work stands singularly alone and apart. **BLAST PRESS** does not take part in the mish-mosh of the magazine market, where a hundred tentative voices are corralled by brute binding into an ersatz herd. We go alone, each of us, to where the crocs swim alertly in the bulrushes and the nights are long. Meet me in Botswana, if you will meet with me at all.

What is a chapbook? A chapbook is a saddle-stapled booklet of plain paper stock folded in half with a sheet of colored card stock for a cover. In the first decade, booklets would be stapled together by hand, each staple closed with a bloody fingertip to save the two-cent per staple cost. All small publishers are unified in this regard: we are exceedingly cheap.

In the next few minutes, for a brief moment, we will hear the voices of some poets that have been published by **BLAST PRESS**. Their words have been put into chapbooks with a **BLAST PRESS** logo on the back, and my current address somewhere inside the front flap. Words torn from the air and swatted into print. That is all. But, that is everything.

Author Ethos

BLAST PRESS is what I would call a "micro-publisher." We usually publish chapbooks—booklets under 100 pages in length. Our print runs are usually under 100 copies per edition. And **BLAST PRESS** has published over 100 chapbooks from some 20 authors in its career. The entire cost is assumed by **BLAST PRESS**, so we are the publisher, and not a vanity press or service.

BLAST PRESS has been sustaining its small operation—in the black, mind you, no small feat—for about 20 years now. We have had a few more ambitious titles where the book itself, the author, and **BLAST PRESS** decide to dedicate the extra resources needed to make the event a success.

Part of the **BLAST PRESS** ethos is to keep the authors in charge of their work so that they can maintain maximum control of their creative material in the out-lying years and don't need to be writing to **BLAST PRESS** for permission to re-publish snippets or poems.

BLAST PRESS catalog available at:
amazon.com/author/gregglory
and gregglory.com

Our Credo

Do not dispraise the light
That, singing whatever's brightest,
Undoes the theft of night—
—Touch to caress, or move to love,
As this thoughtless rhyme does prove.

From **Ascent**

A Solitary Headstone

Niggling addendum to "Meet me in Botswana"

Magazines, published with a week's, month's, quarter's
or even a year's date grow elderly on the shelves in a way that
a collection of one individual's work never can. What year does
Shakespeare's book expire? Horace is renewed year by year,
no matter how worn his saws may wane. But a magazine or
casual collection of miscellaneous artifacts, no matter how
august the individual members of the find, retain an interest
for us mostly as a time capsule.   Even the Egyptian tombs of
the pharaohs hold more interest for us because of what they
reveal about the era of their creation than for what they say
about their putative occupants. Old poetry quarterlies are no
different, although they may contain an Endymion.

This is why **BLAST PRESS** is dedicated to publishing single-author volumes and stand-alone essay collections almost exclusively. Unless a poet is unknown, there is no point in his publication being undertaken by a small press. And if an author is unknown, he is best presented to an unacquainted public in his own exclusive company. It is always wisest to let a guest unroll at least a few of his favorite tales before we escort him from the house. What is characteristic and worthwhile in the poet's voice will quietly assert itself over the course of his varied pieces much better than if we merely heard his alba or evensong in isolation, let alone in the cacophonous squawk of a miscellany. To the marriage of true minds, ours and the author's, let not serial publication admit impediments. Only appearing in magazines and periodicals is like never having a final resting place—a poet without a plot.

BLAST PRESS
324B Matawan Avenue
Cliffwood, NJ 07721
(732) 970-8409
gregglory.com

YOGA NOTES

Yoga Notes

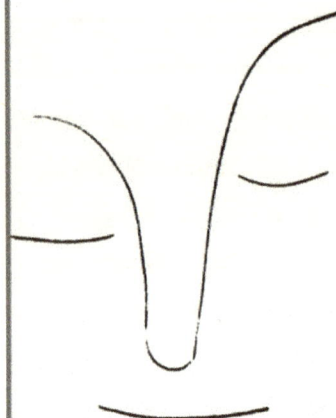

Carrie Pedersen Hudak

List Price: $4.50
5" x 8"
66 pages
ISBN-13: 978-1494330958
ISBN-10: 1494330954
BISAC: Body, Mind & Spirit

CARRIE PEDERSEN HUDAK

From the first essay: Just Practice

When I tell people I am a yoga teacher, they often say, I could never do yoga. I can't even touch my toes. Great, I say, you are already practicing awareness, that's part of the practice. Can you breathe? If you can breathe, then you can do yoga.

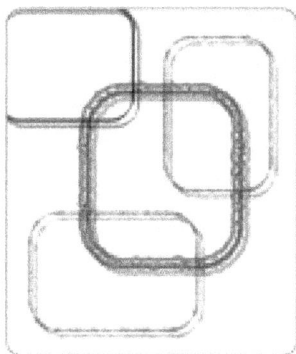

West of Home

Joe Weil, Emily Vogel

List Price: $10.00

Paperback: 98 pages

ISBN-10: 0615878415

ISBN-13:9780615878416

8 x 5 inches

West of Home

Joe Weil and Emily Vogel

From the Introduction

"West of Home" is a collaborative book of poetry which reflects the present and ongoing sentiments of Joe Weil and Emily Vogel. It includes 14 "responsorial" poems (call and response), between the two poets, as they respond to one another's themes and ideas, as well as two sections of poems, one for each poet's individual work.

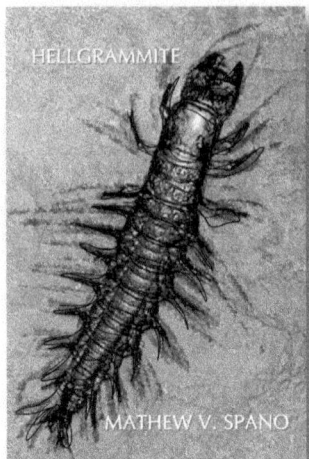

Hellgrammite

Mathew V. Spano

List Price: $9.50
Paperback: 132 pages
ISBN-10: 0692761705
ISBN-13: 978-0692761700
5.5 x 8.5 inches

About Hellgrammite

Hellgrammite" masquerades as a humble book of fishing poems
and tales, but it is much more than that. It is a mythological
multi-legged creature, creeping and crawling with vivid nature
poems, ink drawings, sensitive haiku and two remarkably
crafted short stories. By turns terrifying, tragic, witty and
surreal, author Mathew V. Spano serves as the reader's guide,
turning over river rocks of the unconscious and inviting
readers to reach down into the wet darkness to probe mysteries
of Mother Nature and human nature.

poems by
Daniel Weeks

Self-Symphonies

Daniel Weeks

List Price: $10.00

Paperback: 146 pages

ISBN-10: 0692238581

ISBN-13: 978-0692238585

7.4 x 9.7 inches

From the Introduction

Inspired by listening to the four symphonies of Johannes
Brahms, Daniel Weeks's Self-Symphonies explore the
landscapes, cityscapes, and seascapes that are the backdrop to
a life lived on the New Jersey shore. The four long poems in
this collection provide meditations on family, inheritance, and
loss, society, nature, and culture, and stasis and change–all of
the elements that Coleridge said bething the individual self.

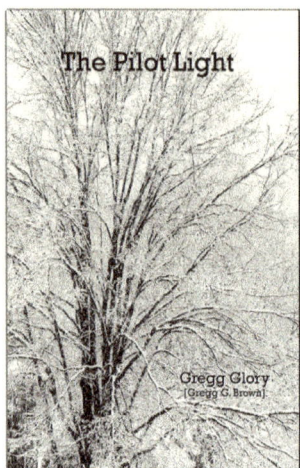

The Pilot Light

Gregg Glory

[Gregg G. Brown]

List Price: $5.50

Paperback: 132 pages

ISBN-13: 9781511941921

5.5 x 8.5 inches

About *The Pilot Light*

The poems in Gregg Glory's The Pilot Light are about
relationships—with family, friends, and lovers—along with
reminiscences of a childhood spent close to nature in the New
Jersey countryside. Glory is particularly adept at exploring the
significant and oftentimes intimate moments that define our
most important relationships, moments which, in turn, help us
create the story of the self.

Knowing the Moment
Emanuel di Pasquale

List Price: $12.95
Paperback: 131 pages
ISBN-13: 9781503117471
5.5 x 8.5 inches

About *Knowing the Moment*

Emanuel di Pasquale has never been one to shy away from the
more difficult aspects of living a full and engaged human life,
and Knowing the Moment is perhaps his most searing work in
this regard, as he confronts the hardships he encountered while
growing up in his native Sicily. But these kinds of revelations
are never the final word in his poetry. Tough times always
seem to point him back to love—as he casts his mind back to life
in Sicily or engages with the present in his poems about Long
Branch, N.J.

THE HUMMINGBIRD'S

A P P R E N T I C E

The Hummingbird's Apprentice

Gregg Glory

[Gregg G. Brown]

List Price: $4.50

Paperback: 159 pages

ISBN-10: 1511941928

ISBN-13: 9781511941921

5.1 x 7.8 inches

GREGG GLORY

From *The Hummingbird's Apprentice*

ROADSIDE WINE

Pull off 71 suddenly, onto

a wide shoulder of dust and grass.

weigh down a length

of brown barbwire fence

like a wave of honey breaking.

Excited, splash ankle-deep

into the unhurrying surf

full of velvety bee sounds, and select

one perfect blossom. It is

so sweet in the slow afternoon.

And, where you've cut your thumb,

a thrill of air catches.

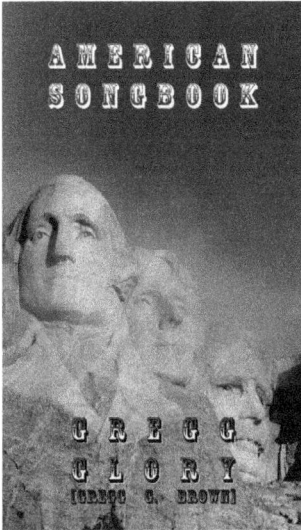

American Songbook

Gregg Glory

[Gregg G. Brown]

List Price: $3.75
Paperback: 98 pages
ISBN-10: 1482703297
ISBN-13: 9780692238585
5.5 x 8.5 inches

The Old Truculence

A note concerning the basic arc of this book of poems—to re-register grace and freedom as America's primary metier.

Freedom breeds elegance. Not the inbred elegance of aristocracy, where beautiful ladies eventually come to resemble their Russian wolfhounds. Nor, simply, the truculent elegance of that sly Benjamin Franklin who, as ambassador to the French Court, refused to bow before King Louis the 16th or doff his coonskin cap.

Freedom breeds the desire to create one meaningful action with your entire life—the effortful elegance of the artist that James Joyce defined as the willingness to gamble your whole life on the wrong idea, a bad aesthetic, or, it may be, a genuine triumph. And America has created, and can still create, a unique scale of opportunity for such elegant "throws of the dice," as Mallarme might say. A natty Fred Astaire (originally Austerlitz), gliding with the ease of an ice skater as he backs Rita Hayworth (a gal from Brooklyn) into immortality to a tune penned by the jewish Jerome Kern in an industry patented in the U.S.A. is but one example of the scale of that opportunity.

When you are free to do anything, a desire grows in the breast not to do just anything, but to do the best thing—and that is an aesthetic dilemma. The mere accumulation of capital, or the arbitrary exercise by minor government regulators of petty power, are two classic examples of the desire for a meaningful expression of life-status that lack the aesthetic instinct. Such timid ambitions grow most strongly where the full range of light is narrowed, and the blossom of selfhood must twist around corners to open its ruby glory in a thinning patch of sunlight.

Gregg Glory
March, 2013

Come, My Dreams

Come gather round me, multitudinous dreams
That in the dim twilight are murmuring soft;
Come lay by my head in the pillow-seam;
Come carry my freighted heart aloft.

O, I would dare dream as few men dream
Beyond the cruel cudgel of the strong,
Beyond the purpled tapestries of is and seems
Hung before my eyes, beyond cold right or wrong.

www.ingramcontent.com/pod-product-compliance
Lightning Source LLC
Chambersburg PA
CBHW031845090426
42741CB00005B/359